What on Earth? Volcanoes

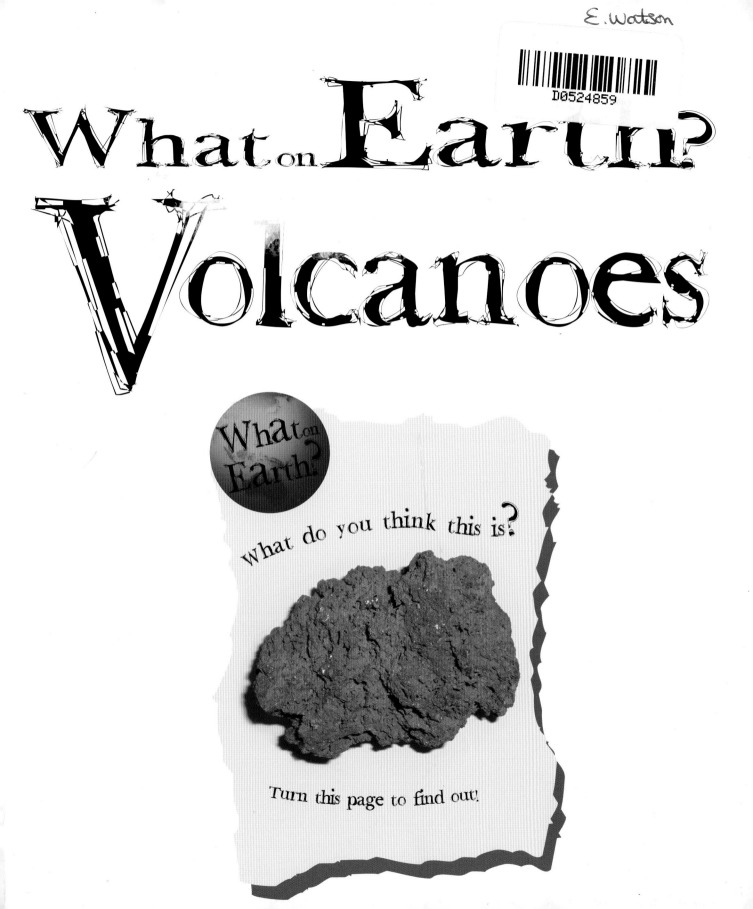

What on Earth?

What do you think this is?

Turn this page to find out!

First published in 2005 by
Book House an imprint of
The Salariya Book Company
25 Marlborough Place
Brighton
BN1 1UB

Please visit The Salariya Book Company at: **www.salariya.com**

HB ISBN 1-905087-29-2
PB ISBN 1-905087-30-6

Visit our website at **www.book-house.co.uk**
for free electronic versions of:
You Wouldn't Want To Be An Egyptian Mummy!
You Wouldn't Want To Be A Roman Gladiator!
You Wouldn't Want to Sail on a 19th-Century Whaling Ship!
Avoid joining Shackleton's Polar Expedition!

Due to the changing nature of internet links, The Salariya Book Company has
developed an online list of websites related to the subject of this book.
This site is updated regularly. Please use this link to access the list:
http://www.book-house.co.uk/WOE/volcanoes

A catalogue record for this book is
available from the British Library.

Printed and bound in China.

Editors:	Ronald Coleman
	Sophie Izod
Senior Art Editor:	Carolyn Franklin
DTP Designer:	Mark Williams

Picture Credits Dave Antram: 8(b), 14(l), 15, 19(t,), 22,
23(m), 24, 25(t), Julian Baker & Janet Baker (J B
Illustrations): 8(t), 9(t), Mark Bergin: 2, 18, 19(b), 19(t),
Elizabeth Branch: 20-21, 24(t), Peter Bull: 16(r), 17(l), Ray
and Corinne Burrows: 14(b), 16(l), Nick Hewetson: 6-7, 12,
23, 25(b), Tony Townsend: 16-17, 26, Jim Sugar /Corbis: 28,
Digital Stock: 9, 23, PhotoDisc: 11, 13, The Salariya Book
Company: 1, 31

Cover credits: PhotoDisc

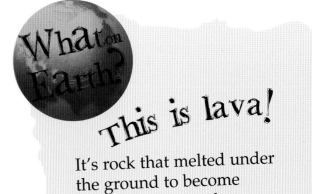

What on Earth?

This is lava!
It's rock that melted under
the ground to become
magma, and was then
pushed out of a volcano.
After that, it's called lava.
Careful! It's sharp!

What on Earth? Volcanoes

Kathryn Senior

Who's this?

Turn to page 19 to find out!

BOOK HOUSE

Contents

What on Earth?

Weird warning!

On May 5th 1902, thousands of snakes invaded the town of St. Pierre on the Caribbean island of Martinique. Three days later the volcano Mount Pelée erupted.

Hissssss

Introduction

Volcanoes form around holes that lead deep below the Earth's surface. Every now and again, molten rock, ash, rocks or gases may force themselves up through the volcano to the surface.

Do all volcanoes look the same?

No. Many volcanoes look like steep mountains, but some are just cracks in the Earth's surface, or are not very high at all. Some volcanoes are islands rising out of the sea, and others are on land.

Do volcanoes erupt very often?

Some volcanoes erupt almost all the time. Others may erupt every few years, or maybe not for hundreds or thousands of years. When a volcano is likely to erupt, we say it is **active**. When it has not erupted for a long time, we say it is dormant. A volcano that has stopped erupting altogether is called extinct.

Why do volcanoes erupt?

Geyser

Volcanoes erupt because of the way that the Earth is formed. Beneath the hard outer crust we live on, there is a layer of very **hot rock**. In places, the rock is so hot that it melts and forces its way up through the crust. This is what is happening when a volcano erupts.

What are plate tectonics?

Earth's crust is made up of huge sections called 'tectonic plates', floating on a layer of molten rock. The plates are always moving and sometimes force each other upwards, forming mountain ranges.

Why are eruptions dangerous?

Molten rock from a volcano is so hot that it burns everything in its path. Many tonnes of rock, ash and burning gases may explode from the top or side of a volcano causing death and destruction.

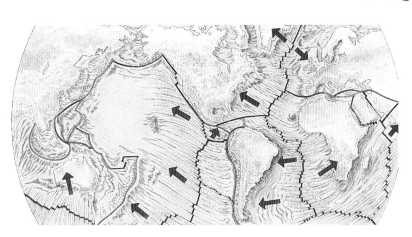

What is magma?

Magma is rock that is so hot that it has become a liquid. Sometimes, it collects in large pools called magma chambers. It is lighter than the harder rock around it, and rises upwards towards Earth's crust. When the magma reaches the surface it is called lava.

Lava

Smoke

Magma chamber

What on Earth?

Old Faithful?

Yellowstone National Park in the USA is home to 'Old Faithful'. This geyser's name comes from the regular spurts of hot water and steam which shoot up in the air.

Whoooooosh!

Where are volcanoes?

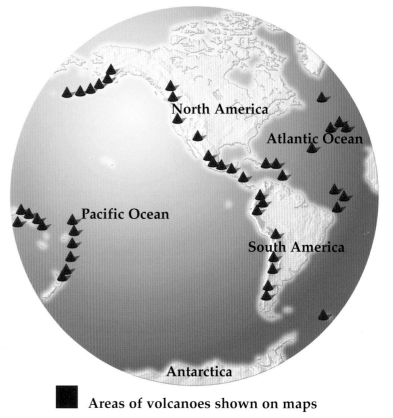

Many of Earth's volcanoes are found along the edges of tectonic plates where the crust is weakest. **Magma** from chambers under the crust forces its way out at these weak points. The maps on these pages show how volcanoes lie in lines along the edges of the plates.

North America

Atlantic Ocean

Pacific Ocean

South America

Antarctica

■ Areas of volcanoes shown on maps

Are there volcanoes near where people live?

Yes, the soil around volcanoes is often very good for growing crops. People start farms, and build homes there. There are farms are on the slopes of Mount Etna in Italy.

What is the 'Pacific Ring of Fire'?

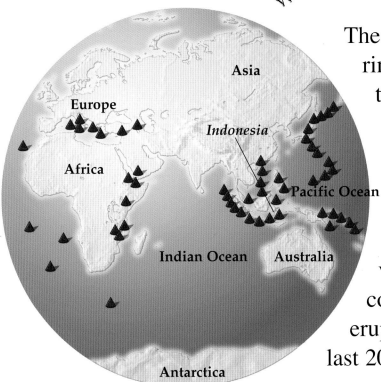

The 'Pacific Ring of Fire' is the ring of volcanoes that surrounds the Pacific Ocean. They are all on the edges of a huge tectonic plate. More than half the world's active volcanoes are found here. Indonesia, at the edge of the plate, has 70 active volcanoes – more than any other country! These volcanoes have erupted more than 600 times in the last 200 years.

Where is Mount Fuji?

Mount Fuji is the highest and most sacred mountain in Japan. It is one of the most beautiful mountains in the world. It is a dormant volcano, which last erupted in 1707.

What happens when a volcano erupts?

Eruptions are not always huge explosions. In fact, some are quite quiet, with thick lava flowing out of the volcano very slowly. If the lava is thin, it is much more dangerous, because it flows faster. Sometimes, lava cools and is thrown out as rocky 'bombs'.

How can we tell if a volcano will erupt?

It's difficult! Sometimes, volcanoes give off smelly gases or start to bulge, but others can erupt without warning.

How long do eruptions last?

Eruptions can be over very quickly – or they may last for years. Stromboli, in Italy has been erupting every few minutes for 2,000 years! A volcano stops erupting when there is no more gas or rock to come out of it. It will also stop if lava cools and makes a plug of rock, so nothing more can escape.

Which is the largest active volcano?

Mauna Loa in Hawaii, is the world's largest volcano. It is a shield volcano, which stands 4,168 metres (13,677 feet) above sea level. Its top is over 8,534 metres (28,000 feet) from the ocean floor.

What kinds of eruption are there?

There are many different kinds of volcanic eruption. Some volcanoes always erupt in the same way, but others may erupt in different ways at different times. Often, the type of **eruption** is named after the volcanoes that usually erupt in those ways. For example, 'Strombolian' eruptions are named after Stromboli, in Italy.

Hawaiian

Hawaiian eruptions are when magma escapes from a crack in Earth's surface, or from a central point.

Pelean

Pelean ('glowing cloud') eruptions are named after Mount Pelée. An explosion of burning gas, dust and ash races down the mountain.

Strombolian

In Strombolian eruptions huge amounts of molten lava burst from the crater, making sparks in the sky.

Vulcanian

Vulcanian eruptions (named after Vulcano, see page 18) are when gas and ash explode from the crater forming a cloud near the volcano's top.

Plinian

In Plinian eruptions (named after a Roman writer), thick lava, ash and gas explode high into the air.

What is a shield volcano?

In a shield volcano, lava pours out of one or more vents (cracks) in Earth's crust. Lava flows out in all directions and hardens. Over hundreds of years, this builds up a broad, sloping cone, like a warrior's shield.

Shield volcano
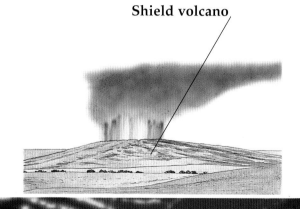

What's the most dangerous?

Pelean eruptions are the most dangerous. Hot, dry rocks and burning gases pour down the mountain very fast. This is called a 'pyroclastic flow'. One of the most famous eruptions ever was when Mount Vesuvius in Italy, erupted in AD 79 and destroyed three towns: Pompeii, Herculaneum and Stabiae. Many thousands of people died, but we can still see the ruins of the cities today.

The best place to be?

In 1902, a prisoner in an underground cell was one of only two people to survive when Mount Pelée in Martinique destroyed the town of St. Pierre.

Why are volcanoes important?

Volcanoes are very important to us, even though they can cause so much **damage** because they change the land around them. Sometimes they form new mountains or new islands. Volcanic rocks are full of useful metals, such as copper, silver and gold, and may also contain gemstones such as diamonds.

What's this?

Vulcanologists use special probes like this to collect samples of lava

Why do people study volcanoes?

Scientists called 'vulcanologists' study volcanoes. They try to find out why and when they will erupt. This can save many lives.

How do vulcanologists stay safe?

Vulcanologists have to get very close to study volcanoes and temperatures can reach 1000°C (1832°F). This means they must wear special protective suits and helmets.

Phew! Wow!

Why take photographs?

Filming volcanoes helps scientists study the different kinds of eruption, and learn more about how people can stay safe.

Vulcanologist

What on Earth?

Rocks in the bath?

Lava sometimes contains a special kind of rock called pumice. It is very light, and very rough. People can use it to rub away hard skin from their hands and feet.

Scrub! Scrub!

How old are volcanoes?

Volcanoes have been around almost as long as planet Earth. The oldest rocks on Earth date from nearly four **billion** years ago. Scientists studying these can tell that there were volcanoes all that time ago, and see how these, earthquakes and moving tectonic plates have shaped our world.

Where did this rock come from?

This church in eastern France was built on a volcanic plug. The volcano became extinct and wore away. Only the plug remains.

Who put these rocks here?

These rocks in Northern Ireland are called the 'Giant's Causeway'. There is a legend that a giant put them there. In fact they formed from lava around 55-65 million years ago.

What happens when tectonic plates move?

Magma bubbles up and escapes through weak places in Earth's crust

Volcanoes erupt where tectonic plates move apart

How do volcanoes change the earth?

New rocks form when lava erupts from volcanoes at the edges of the tectonic plates. In other places, rocks are forced down beneath the crust as the plates push against each other, often causing earthquakes.

How did volcanoes kill sea life?

Around 250 million years ago, volcanoes in Siberia pumped out about 10 billion tonnes of carbon dioxide. This caused global warming. Four-fifths of all sea life died, and it took five million years for Earth to recover.

Lava from volcanoes under the sea hardens and becomes part of Earth's crust

A volcano's vent is like a chimney, leading deep into the Earth which magma travels up

Did we always understand volcanoes?

Today, we have a lot of scientific information about volcanoes. In the past, volcanoes were **mysterious** and frightening, so people made up stories to explain them.
All over the world there were different myths and legends to explain volcanoes.

What are these crosses?

They are rock crystals formed when Mount Vesuvius erupted in 1660. People thought they were a message from God.

How did volcanoes get their name?

The name 'volcano' comes from the Roman god Vulcan. The Romans believed Vulcan was a blacksmith, who made weapons for other gods. His forge was under the island of Vulcano, near Sicily.

Crash!

Bang!

Bang! Crash!

Clang!

How did a warrior become a volcano?

A story from the Aztec people of Mexico tells of a warrior who fell in love with the Emperor's daughter. When they died, the gods turned them into mountains. The warrior became the volcano Popocatépetl.

Who is Pele?

Pele was the Hawaiian goddess of volcanoes and fire. Hawaiians believed she lived in the volcano Kilauea. They said that Pele caused earthquakes by stamping her feet, and volcanic eruptions by striking the ground with a stick.

What on Earth?

Who lives on Kilimanjaro?

Kilimanjaro, in Tanzania, is a dormant volcano. It is around 6,000 metres (19,000 feet) above sea level, and is the highest mountain in Africa. No one lives at the snow covered top, but the lower slopes have been home to farmers for thousands of years.

The end of life?

A big eruption can destroy everything around it. Lava and hot ash burn the plants and kill the animals. However, the land recovers amazingly quickly. After Mount St. Helens in the USA erupted in 1980, everything looked **black** and **dead**. But weeks later, tiny insects zoomed in – about two million of them every day. Beetles came to eat the insects, accidentally bringing in plant seeds. Twenty five years later, the land has almost recovered.

What's so special about volcanic soil?

Volcanic soil is very rich in the minerals that plants need to grow well. Where there are many plants, there are also many animals. For example, the beautiful Hawaiian islands were formed from volcanoes. Huge numbers of plants grow there, and many animals live among the plants.

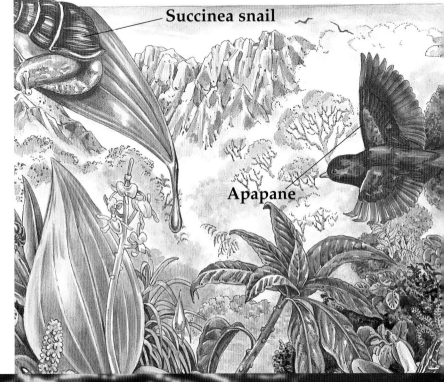

Succinea snail

Apapane

What grows first?

Lichens begin to grow on lava after an eruption.

They provide shelter for insects and other small creatures.

Mosses start to grow. Over time, the soil gets thicker and then larger plants grow.

Who hopped in?

Small frogs were among the first animals to live near Mount St. Helens after the eruption. The frogs turned up near mossy pools, just three years after the lava had cooled.

Hop! Hop! Hop!

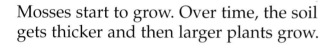

Hawaiian damselfly

Kamehameha butterfly

Hawaiian goose

Iiwi

Can we tell if a volcano is extinct?

Sometimes it is very hard to tell if a volcano is extinct or dormant. A volcano can appear to be inactive for hundreds or thousands of years, then suddenly burst into action. In 1991, Mount Pinatubo in the Philippines had not erupted for 400 years, so when scientists warned people nearby of the danger many did not take any notice. When the eruption came, more than 300 people died.

Why do people get hurt?

Volcanoes can do damage in unexpected ways. When Mount St. Helens erupted in 1980, no one expected the huge mud flows that came down the mountain. Fifty-seven people died in these.

Will Mount Fuji erupt?

More than 12 million people live near Mount Fuji in Japan. An eruption could cause huge damage, so the Japanese government is spending millions of dollars to find ways to predict an eruption and protect people.

Is this volcano dangerous?

Mount Rainier, in northwest USA, is an active volcano. An eruption here could affect the city of Seattle, which is only about 100 kilometres (60 miles) away.

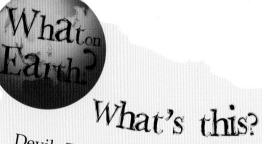

What on Earth?

What's this?

Devils Tower in Wyoming was once part of a volcano. It is formed from a steep tower of lava that cooled around 40 million years ago. It is around 380 metres (1,250 feet) tall.

Volcanoes under the sea?

There are around 5,000 active volcanoes under the sea. Some have burst through the surface to become islands. Hawaii is one of these. It is part of a volcanic ridge, formed from a 'hot spot' of magma deep underground. It has been pushing through Earth's crust for at least 70 million years.

An underwater vent

What's the Hawaiian Ridge?

The Hawaiian Ridge is a chain of volcanoes in the Pacific Ocean. It is over 2,400 kilometres (1,500 miles) long - the world's longest chain.

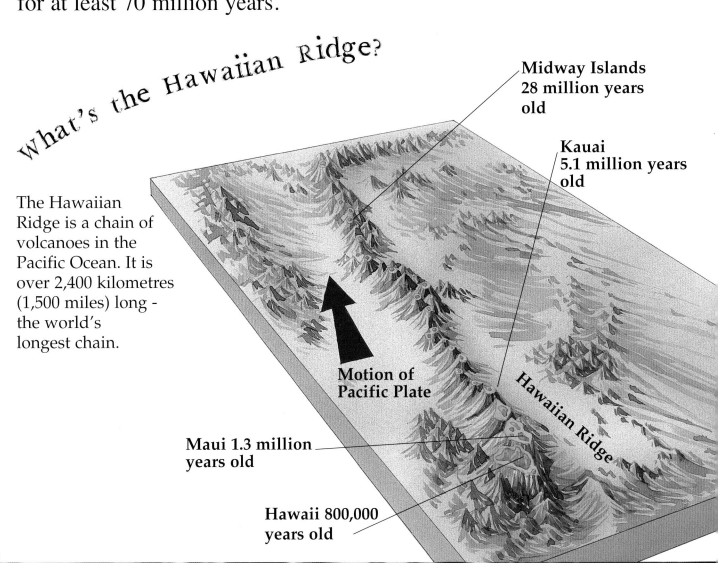

Midway Islands 28 million years old

Kauai 5.1 million years old

Motion of Pacific Plate

Hawaiian Ridge

Maui 1.3 million years old

Hawaii 800,000 years old

What are atolls?

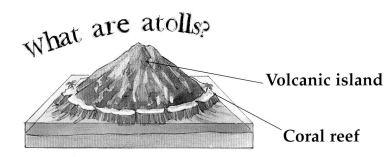

Volcanic island

Coral reef

An atoll is created when a coral reef, made from the skeletons of tiny sea creatures, forms around a volcanic island.

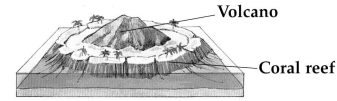

Volcano

Coral reef

After a while, the volcano sinks into the sea. Meanwhile, more coral has formed. In the end, the volcano disappears altogether but the round coral island remains.

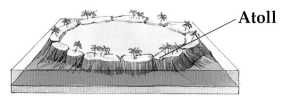

Atoll

What on Earth?

Is there hot water under the sea?

There are few living things in the deepest oceans, except near 'hydrothermal vents'. These are like geysers under the sea. Water, heated by magma under Earth's crust, flows up into the sea.

Mmmm... cosy!

What's a tsunami?

A tsunami is a series of waves caused by an undersea volcanic eruption or earthquake. They can travel in the open sea as fast as 450 kilometres (280 miles) an hour. As they reach the coast they can grow to 30 metres (100 feet) high. A tsunami in South-East Asia on December 26th, 2004 killed over 200,000 people.

Volcanoes on other planets?

In our solar system, only Earth and Venus have active volcanoes but there are extinct volcanoes on Mars. Most are on **huge** domes in regions called Tharsis and Elysium. The Tharsis dome is 4,000 kilometres (2,500 miles) across and 10 kilometres (6 miles) high. It has three large shield volcanoes: Ascraeus Mons, Pavonis Mons and Arsia Mons.

Is this a moon?

Yes it's Io, one of the moons of the planet Jupiter. Its surface is covered with lava flows, lava lakes and geysers full of sulphur. Volcanic eruption plumes rise 100 kilometres (62 miles) high.

Volcanic plume

What on Earth volcanic Venus?

In the 1990s, the Magellan spacecraft found 168 huge volcanoes on Venus, nearly 300 medium-sized ones and hundreds of thousands of smaller ones. Only one, Maat Mons, is definitely active.

How would you survive a volcanic eruption?

Erupting volcanoes are not the only sign of volcanic activity. The magnificent natural fountains, or geysers of steam and hot water in the USA, Iceland and New Zealand are all linked to volcanic activity.

Volcano Dangers

Burning Lava can reach temperatures of 1250°C (2282°F) and travel at over 113 kph (70 mph). Get in a car and drive away as quickly as possible!

Being Buried 30 cm (12 inches) of ash is enough to collapse a roof. If possible keep your roof clear of ash.

Poisoning Store drinking water in baths or containers, as the water supply may become polluted.

what to do Check-list

Wear a gas mask so you can breathe and wear a pair of goggles to protect your eyes from thick ash. Don't leave the house, unless the ash is thick on the roof and it looks like collapsing. Shut all windows and doors so none of the ash can get in. Take off outdoor clothing to remove ash and keep a first-aid kit to treat burns.

Other, less dramatic signs are the bubbling pools of hot, thick volcanic mud which often occur near geysers. 'Smokers' are geysers that occur on the seabed, usually where two tectonic plates meet.

Volcano facts

Earth's crust is between 25 km (15 miles) and 70 km (47 miles) thick. Under the oceans, the crust is a lot thinner – only 7 km (4 miles) thick in some places.

It can take years for lava from a volcano to cool. In Mexico, there is a volcano where people can still light sticks of wood from lava that erupted over 40 years ago!

In Japan, there are springs of hot water where monkeys like to bathe in winter to keep warm.

In 1963, scientists in Iceland watched a new island being formed. A volcano erupted under the sea and soon created an island that rose 169 metres (515 feet) above sea level and had an area of 2.5 square kilometres (nearly 1 square mile). They called it 'Surtsey', after 'Surtur' the Norse fire giant.

Some volcanoes on Mars are over three billion years old. The youngest ones are about 200 million years old but they are all extinct.

Glossary

Active A volcano that could erupt at any time.

Carbon dioxide A kind of gas.

Crystal A rock that has formed into a regular shape, such as a square.

Dormant A volcano that has not erupted for a long time.

Extinct A volcano that will never erupt again.

Gemstone A jewel stone, such as a diamond.

Geyser A fountain of natural hot water.

Hot spot A pocket of magma in Earth's outer layer (its crust).

Hydrothermal vent A spring of hot water under the sea.

Magma Rock from deep in Earth's crust that is so hot it has melted.

Plug Magma that has formed a solid block in the centre of a volcano.

Pyroclastic flow Hot ash and gas that pours down the side of a volcano.

Tectonic plate A section of Earth's crust.

Tsunami A series of huge waves caused by an earthquake or volcano.

Vent The hole in the centre of a volcano.

Vulcanologist A scientist who studies volcanoes.

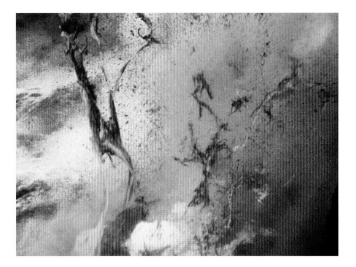

What do you know about volcanoes?

1   What do we call a volcano that will never erupt again?

2   What's the difference between magma and lava?

3   Where is the Pacific Ring of Fire?

4   What's a pyroclastic flow?

5   What's a vulcanologist?

6   Who was Vulcan?

7   Where is Popocatépetl?

8   Is Mount Pinatubo in the Philippines extinct?

9   Where's the world's biggest volcano?

10 What's an atoll?

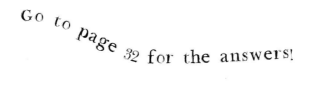

Go to page 32 for the answers!

What is this ?

Index

Pictures are shown in **bold** type.

Answers

1 An extinct volcano. (See page 22)
2 Magma is the melted rock found below Earth's surface. It is called lava when it reaches the surface. (See page 7)
3 Along the edges of the Pacific Ocean. (See page 9)
4 Hot, dry rocks and burning gases which pour down a volcano. (See page 13)
5 A scientist who studies volcanoes. (See page 14)
6 A Roman god. (See page 18)
7 Mexico. (See page 19)
8 No! It's dormant. (See page 22)
9 Mauna Loa, in Hawaii. (See page 11)
10 A coral reef formed around a volcano. (See page 25)

It's a 'volcanic bomb'. Blobs of lava are thrown out of the volcano and some solidify in the air, landing as 'bombs' on the ground.